The Secret of His Presence

W. Phillip Keller

SONGTIME, INC.
BOX 350
BOSTON, MASS. 02101

HARVEST HOUSE PUBLISHERS
Eugene, Oregon 97402

Except where otherwise indicated, Scripture quotations in this book are taken from the King James Version of the Bible.

THE SECRET OF HIS PRESENCE

Taken from **PREDATORS IN OUR PULPITS**
Copyright © 1988 by Harvest House Publishers
Eugene, Oregon 97402

ISBN 0-89081-730-8

All rights reserved. No portion of this book may be reproduced in any form without the written permission of the Publisher.

Printed in the United States of America.

Contents

**The Call
to Surrender**
5

**Positioning
Our Priorities**
14

Simplifying Our Lives
21

A Renewed Allegiance
30

**Our High and
Noble Calling**
38

1
The Call to Surrender

If any person is going to follow Christ in wholehearted allegiance, he must clearly understand His character. It simply is not enough for us to be told about His actions in a historical narrative. Jesus the Christ is not just a person who came on the scene as another prophet and spent a few brief years among men being abused, as most prophets are.

He is the very person of God, who is from everlasting to everlasting, without beginning and without termination. He is God, very God, all-knowing, all-wise, all-powerful, who of His own will set His celestial splendors aside and took on Himself for a few brief years our human form. His was a perfect life, lived out in an impeccable character, with a sinless personality. This life He laid down deliberately in an act of enormous generosity to provide the perfect sacrifice of self-giving to propitiate for the awesome evil of all men everywhere. In demonstration of His own perfection and divine power He rose in utter triumph from the tomb. Death could not deter Him. Decomposition could not defile Him. Despair could not diminish His dynamic, eternal life. In utter majesty He ascended again to His position of power and prominence in the infinite realm of the unseen-yet-everlasting spiritual world. He is ever alive!

Jesus Christ came among us but briefly, yet in those few short years He revealed to us the essential character of God. He was the living embodiment of all those qualities which make life lovely, noble, joyous, and worthwhile. Amid the mayhem of man's despair, delusion, and darkness, He it is who always comes with hope, utter integrity, truth, and bright light.

For want of a better word in our human language the Spirit of God has chosen to call Him *love*. Yet He is not love in the mere sense of something sentimental, sweet, and rather romantic (though devotion to Him can arouse such sensations in the human soul) but much more. Yes, much more—more than can be found anywhere in the human family . . . enduring compassion and utter comprehension.

In Christ it is possible for us to both see and understand the wonder and the winsomeness of God's character. Its unique quality, which is so totally foreign to us earthlings, is its utter selflessness. In Christ we see the essence of a self-giving spirit. We can discern, even if only faintly, what it means to be self-sharing, self-sacrificing, and self-losing for the good of others in a continuous outpouring of life that is laid down for the well-being of others.

This gracious, magnanimous self-giving is the distinctive dynamic of Christ's love. It is the essential energy of His being. It is the powerful influence of His Person which counteracts all the evil, sin, and selfishness of human society.

It follows, then, that when He calls us into His company it is expected of us that we too shall become people of that caliber. His supreme desire is that those who are to be His people should display the same qualities of character which He does. If we are to call ourselves Christians ("like Christ"), then it is incumbent upon us to be like Christ not only in our outward conduct but also in our inmost character.

Christ spoke much about the "glory of God." He longed to share it with His associates. He prayed the Father to bestow it upon His followers as He Himself had revealed it to them. This "glory of God" is nothing else but the very character of Christ. His impeccable character is His supreme glory. It is His unique caliber of life and conduct which set Him apart from and far above His creation.

So when the Master invited men and women to come to Him and to follow Him, He was in truth calling them to an entirely new sort of life. The old ways would no longer do. The old attitudes would have to change. The old selfish, self-centered character would have to be completely altered.

In the very plain, simple, blunt language of His day He stated categorically, "If any man will come after me, let him deny himself and take up his cross daily and follow me" (Luke 9:23).

This implies clearly that to be in His company and walk in harmony with Him, having the same aims and objectives as He does, must entail self-denial. It sounds so simple to say, but it is the most difficult thing in all the world to do. It is a formidable cost to consider!

If we are to be allied with Christ, then obviously we cannot be in antagonism to Him. There can be no accord between His sublime selflessness and our petty, personal self-centeredness. Our selfishness must go. Our self-preoccupation has to be put to death. Our self-will has to be sacrificed to His great, generous goodwill!

This inherent human selfishness, which He commands us to abandon, finds expression in scores of different ways. Here are but a few: self-assertion, self-adulation, self-interest, self-pity, self-indulgence, self-gratification, self-avengement. These smooth, high-sounding terms so much esteemed by our human society are translated into rather startling language by God's Spirit in the Scriptures. There they are called "the works of the flesh"—namely adultery, fornication, lewdness, idolatry, hatred, dissension, wrath, anger, strife, seditions, envy, jealousy, etc.

It is common for human beings to object strongly to such a demand. They insist that they are just "doing what comes naturally" when they live this way. That is true—it is just the corrupt old human character. They insist they were simply born that way. That is true too! Man is born in sin and his whole personality is shaped in iniquity. They claim they can't help themselves. Nor can they! That is why they must come to Christ. They must cast themselves upon His compassion. They must trust Him to turn them around. And He will if they will it so.

Here is where the crunch comes.

Do we truly want to be different? Do we long to be remade in His likeness? Do we earnestly wish to be changed from our old character, so defiled, to His, so pure?

These are searching questions for the soul of man. They penetrate to the very center of his being. They call for radical and drastic changes in a person. They demand a complete re-creation of character.

The price to pay is daily self-denial.

The cost is to relinquish self-will to Christ's will.

The process is a painful crucifixion of one's self-centeredness in order to be free from self to follow Christ in love and joyous abandon.

Christ's call for us to renounce our self-interests in order to follow Him at first appears an impossible price to pay. This is because it entails total surrender. But the deep decision to do this can be accelerated when we begin to see clearly that we are slaves to ourselves. We are literally in bondage to our own crude, selfish, arrogant self-approbation. And this is really the source of most of our sorrow, stress, and pain in life. Oh, to be set free from the sinister shackles of our own self-interests! We are actually held captive by our own ego, pride, and self-esteem.

Christ comes to us and offers to set us free from our self-imprisonment. He sets the captive free to follow Him in glad self-renunciation. He breaks the bonds that bind us to ourselves and lets us take the high road of holiness with Him.

The reverse side of the challenge put to us is to discover the joy, beauty, and abundant delight to be found in doing Christ's commands. By degrees it dawns upon our dull spiritual awareness that none of His demands are to demean us or drive us into despair. Quite the opposite! Each is designed for our good. They are to enrich our lives, enlarge our experience, broaden our horizons, and enhance our well-being. They are actually for our maximum living. Consequently it becomes an honor and high calling to comply with His wishes. He becomes our very inspiration!

When this realization sweeps over our spirits it carries away our spiritual blindness as to what Christ's noble intentions are toward us. What from our old perspective appeared to be an enormous price of self-sacrifice can now be understood as a most special honor bestowed upon us by God, inviting us to come into His exclusive company. We see clearly that Christ is challenging us to a lofty life like His own, in which He calls us His companions, His friends, and yes, even more—His brothers and sisters.

For His part, He is fully prepared to enter any life opened to Him. He is ready to share Himself fully with any soul (person) who will receive Him as The Most High Majesty. He is delighted to take up residence within any human being who will in humility open up the innermost sanctum of his or her will and disposition to His presence.

On our part He asks that deliberately and very consistently we submit ourselves to His control. As this is done daily, it is He who empowers us to carry out His commands and to comply with His wishes. Our wholehearted compliance with His will is made possible because of our implicit confidence in His superb character. He will not delude or defraud us. He is totally trustworthy, so all is well.

This simple faith in His impeccable faithfulness to us opens up a whole wide world of joyous adventure with Him. We discover that as we deliberately make ourselves totally available to His noble purposes upon the planet, we are caught up with Him in joyous service and projects beyond our fondest hopes. He takes our little lives and uses them to His own great ends.

The sacrifice of self no longer looms large and costly in our calculations. Now we see it as our very reasonable response to the overtures of His love and concern for us. We begin to love as He loves, because He first loved us. We begin to grasp the eternal truth that the chief end of man is not to serve himself but to please Christ and to benefit others. We begin to see here the secret to serenity, the key to contentment, the dynamic for abundant living.

Day by day as by a deliberate act of our wills we choose to conform to Christ's wishes, to align ourselves with His aspirations, to cultivate His companionship, and to relish His presence within, we stumble over another great secret: He is simultaneously at work within us by His Spirit, conforming us to His own exquisite character. An exciting exchange is going on within our spirits, our souls, our very bodies. We are being recreated, remade into selfless, gracious, generous, great-hearted people. We are different, distinct, and separate from the self-oriented society around us.

The distinction does not lie in our adherence to some special creed or set of legal obligations. The difference lies in the dynamic of Christ's life within us and around us. He it is who now determines our deportment. We are no longer our own; we are His. Our conduct, our conversation, our characters are a living witness that He has complete command of our lives. What an honor! WHAT A HIGH AND NOBLE CALLING!

2
Positioning Our Priorities

The person who sincerely sets his will to be the Master's man or woman very quickly comes to see that Christ calls for a profound change in life's priorities. To put it in the plainest language, He not only demands a change of conduct, of character, and of conversation, but also of career. At least the place of prominence given to our careers in our everyday decisions has to be altered.

In the contemporary church with its worldly view of self-affirmation and self-fulfillment the challenge to sacrifice our careers for Christ is seldom mentioned. The more popular approach made to the masses by their leaders is that Christianity is a social activity that is sort of added on to one's secular career. It is hoped, of course, that this can be done with a minimum of disturbance to the daily activities demanded by one's normal lifestyle. It is seldom stated that to follow Christ calls for a radical upheaval in one's priorities, whatever they may be. This entails drastic dislocation of our devotion to those interests which formerly held first place in our day-to-day considerations.

This is a catastrophic challenge which very few people are prepared to accept. The cost seems too prohibitive, the sacrifice too severe. After all, it is argued that an individual may have spent the best years of his youth and huge sums of money in preparation for his life profession. Or he may have invested enormous amounts of time, energy, and concentration in qualifying for a certain career of his own choosing. Or through long years of apprenticeship, hard work, and excruciating experiences he may have reached a certain level of excellence in his field of endeavor. Surely he is not going to be asked to set all of this aside in order to do Christ's bidding!

If we turn our attention to the few brief years of our Lord's public life among His contemporaries, we are startled to see that this is what He demanded. He spoke to men like Matthew and Zaccheus. They were tough, hard-driving tax collectors who had amassed wealth through the corruption so common in their culture. There had to be a change. They had to leave the old life behind.

Jesus the Christ came into the lives of women like Mary Magdalene, who had plied her profession as a prostitute, and Martha, the house-proud homemaker. For both of these ladies at the extreme opposite ends of the social spectrum the Master called for a dramatic and daring change of career and concern.

To our natural minds such demands may impress us as being too drastic, too devastating. We may even feel that it is going too far for Him to ask us to alter our course in life, to sacrifice the skills and experience which mean so much to us.

The legitimate and pressing question may be asked, "Why?"

The answer is really quite simple. It is in two parts. The first is that obviously if most of our time, energy, thought, and skills are devoted to our own personal ends, they cannot be available to His highest purposes for us. Secondly, no matter how noble or fine our profession or duties may be, if accomplished by our own experience, skill, training, or industry they offer no opportunity for Christ to demonstrate what He can do in us and through us.

It calls for confidence in Christ to respond to His call and step out of the regular old routine. It is a ringing challenge to our faith in God to forsake the familiar life patterns of our professions or careers to step out into new fields of service for Him. It involves unshakable trust in His character that we will dare to cut off the old systems that supported us in order to do His will and accomplish His work under the guidance of His Spirit.

Part of the painful price to pay for such bold faith is the cruel taunts of our contemporaries. We will be charged with being eccentric. Some of us will be branded as fanatics. Others will be referred to as "religious kooks" out of step with the times. Even within the church there will be those who sneer at such a sacrifice.

Yet for the person brave enough to make this break with the contemporary scene of his career there are great compensations. Christ will become exceedingly precious as a constant companion. He will endow the individual with unusual capacities to carry out His wishes. He will empower the follower to accomplish tasks never dreamed of before. He will energize the disciple to impact people that otherwise would not be touched by the life of Christ.

This is because priorities have been reversed and Christ has been given supreme preeminence in the life.

Sometimes such a turnaround takes place in a simple, startling decision of the will to capitulate completely to Christ. At other times it is an ongoing process that proceeds over a period of months or years, often in fits and starts. Little by little more and more of one's time, interests, career, and enthusiasm are turned over to the Master exclusively for His use to the benefit of others as the Holy Spirit graciously guides.

One of the astonishing discoveries that attends this relinquishment of our priorities to Christ is that in many, many instances the same interests and enthusiasm which bound us before are returned to us in a transmuted form. Instead of being indulged for personal self-fulfillment or self-advancement, those skills, talents, capacities, and experience are now exercised for the benefit, inspiration, and uplift of others.

We are no longer shackled into servitude to ourselves. We are set free to use all our skills to serve Christ and bring enormous blessing to our associates. What before bound us into the narrow confines of merely trying to attain our own aims and satisfy our own selfish aspirations is suddenly scattered wide, flung free from our open hands to enrich our generation. We no longer live just for our own fame or fortune, but we live to honor Christ and to promote His purposes on the planet.

The layperson who determines above all things to do Christ's bidding, to come under His control, to submit wholeheartedly to the Sovereign Saviour, is inevitably placed in a position of tension between two opposite principles: that of God's will, which is to give and give and give, and that of the world's way, which is to get and get and get. Christ calls us to be generous. Society insists that we be greedy. Christ challenges us to lose our lives for others. Our culture cries out for us to save ourselves at any cost.

If the Christian is utterly honest, he must admit that the entire world system in which he is present is set on grasping all it can. Its ultimate aims are ease, accumulation of wealth, financial security, self-aggrandizement, social or academic prestige, and personal prominence or power in all their diverse and multifaceted forms.

The individual's energy, strength, time, attention, skills, experience, and career are all dedicated to these ends. The more he succeeds in achieving them, the more he is applauded for his accomplishments.

Standing in bold and stark contradistinction to this world view is Christ's outlook on life. He tells us to give to others, to share what we have, to bless those in need. His measure is to go the second mile even with difficult people. We are to share not only the comfortable outer coat but even the shirt off our back if need be. He asks us to extend mercy, justice, and truth even to those who want to tear us to pieces.

This is a tall order indeed. But the person prepared to lay down his or her own aims and ambitions for others, to sacrifice himself to save others, to lose his own life in finding the lost, to forsake his own fame and fortune in order to benefit his generation, to let go gladly of his career and ambitions for the good of those less fortunate—such a person will stumble over an incredible discovery: This is the way to enormous contentment in life! It is the way to find profound purpose in living, the way to find inward dignity and great honor not because of *who* we are but because of *whose* we are! We are His; we belong to Him. We are in *Christ's company*, and all is well. It is a profound paradox, but it is eternally true.

People who are willing to sacrifice their priorities and allow Christ to reverse their values will discover in actual fact that what He says is so: "Whosoever shall seek to save his life shall lose it, and whosoever shall lose his life shall preserve it" (Luke 17:33).

This is the secret to abundant living in compliance with the will and wishes of Christ. The more we pour out upon others, the more He pours into our daily experience from the bounty of His own infinite supply. His presence, His power, His Person provide all we need. It is no longer "I" but rather "HE" who lives in me!

3
Simplifying Our Lives

The so-called "American dream" has always been one of the great driving forces in the history of our people. It has long been considered one of the fundamental rights of the residents of this continent for each person, regardless of origin or background, to become prosperous and wealthy. The old European traditions of being born into a certain class, and therefore destined to remain there, were blown away in the powerful winds of freedom that formed our societies.

It has always been regarded a profound privilege for anyone willing to work hard and apply his or her initiative to the immense natural resources of the continent to accumulate considerable private possessions. With this wealth came the power, influence, and freedom to do very much as one wished.

In all of this the acquisition of possessions assumes an all-important part of life. In actual fact, materialism has in large measure become a way of life.

Owning a home, property, all the finest furnishings, a luxury car, expensive clothes, and elegant food are considered a normal aspiration within reach of the masses. Beyond these it has also been considered appropriate to have substantial bank holdings, monetary investments, and other financial securities which form a network of security amid the ups and downs of the economic scene which is so unpredictable.

So it is not surprising that in our culture a fairly large measurement of a man and woman's "success" is in terms of their possessions. What kind of home do they own? What model car do they drive? What sort of clothes do they wear? What quality of furnishings do they buy? How flush is their financial position? Where do they go for their holidays? What scholastic credentials do they hold? And so the long list goes on in our subconscious minds.

Of course industry, business, and commerce, using all the persuasive powers of the media, coupled with high-pressure advertising, continually fuel the fires of our desires. They play upon our vanity to urge us to acquire all we can. This is the bedrock of business. We have become the most consumer-oriented society ever known. We are bedazzled by ten thousand items of trade and commerce displayed in ten thousand tantalizing ways to attract our attention and fuel our passion for possession.

In very smooth and subtle ways we become convinced that our lives really do consist in the abundance of things we possess. We are sure that the end result of our education, experience, and expertise in earning a salary are to be dedicated to the acquisition of wealth, security, and ease. We are satisfied that the supreme end of man is to be comfortable and secure amid his personal possessions.

In view of the foregoing, the vast majority of people consider it perfectly proper to have their predominant aims and ambitions in life grounded in material gain. From our earliest years, as tiny tots, we have set before us the role model of adults caught up in the feverish scramble to get ahead, to get more, to get to the top of the totem pole. Enormous thought, time, energy, and expertise are devoted to "piling it up." Because of the selfish nature of people they are seldom contented with just the first million—there must be a second, then a third. All of this becomes a grim game with no holds barred, in which people play for keeps using almost any advantage available to them, whether honest or not.

The end result has been to consider profit and advancement the bottom line in life. Little thought is given to the ethics of courtesy, decency, integrity, or generosity. These are all considered expendable in order to make a buck and gain ground.

If we turn our attention to the personal life and public pronouncements of Jesus

Christ we must be shocked and startled by the difference in His aims and ambitions. It is of more than passing interest that by far the greater portion of His years were spent in quiet, diligent labor as a common carpenter craftsman. There can be no doubt that He produced excellent workmanship, for He was well-known in Nazareth. He saw this work as His own proper responsibility to support His widowed mother and younger siblings. His Father above saw it too, and was well-pleased.

Quite obviously He never amassed the proceeds from His profession as a means to provide for His own ease, comfort, or wealth. He later let it be known that He did not even have a home, though foxes had dens and birds had nests. Even at the end of His short life He left no estate. He apparently owned only the common clothes of the common people—which were stripped from Him by His executioners.

Repeatedly in public He urged His hearers not to become preoccupied with such ordinary possessions as food, drink, clothing, and housing. His assurance was that anyone who put God's interests first would in fact be provided for adequately. He stated categorically that "a man's life does not consist in the abundance of things which he possesses."

When would-be disciples came to Him seeking to join His ranks and become His followers, He made the basic terms tough—at least from our soft perspective they appear that way. He told the rich young man to first go and sell all he possessed and give it to the poor, and then follow Him! He told the one with the field to forget about it. If he had set his hand to the plow there was no looking back to his possession! Always one had to count the cost of following Christ in sacrificing possessions.

In His account of the well-to-do farmer who decided to build larger barns and increase his assets so that he could take it easy, eat, drink, and be merry, He declared the man to be an utter fool. His aims and aspirations were completely self-centered and consequently of no eternal worth to either God or others. He had established no credit with God!

These are drastic indictments, and they should sober up people whose main preoccupation is to amass possessions. On the other hand, Christ made it clear through His use of parables about the stewards and the talents entrusted to them that we are held responsible for our capacities to accumulate and manage possessions.

For Christians there are basic principles which need to be grasped if they are to use wealth wisely in the way the Master wishes.

The first of these is to recognize in genuine humility that every capacity (whether of mind, body, personality, or energy) entrusted to us for earning and accumulating possessions is a gift from God our Father. We are not self-made people, as so many suppose! Even the bounties of our natural resources are bestowed upon us in abundance by our gracious God as a generous outpouring of His provision.

It follows then that we are not little deities who in pride and pomp can parade our wealth as an indicator of prestige. Nor are we entitled to be selfish little dictators who decide entirely what we shall do with our talents, time, and assets. Rather, we are to see ourselves as humble stewards of The Most High Majesty, entrusted with His largess, which is to be used for His honor and the benefit of His beneficiaries.

We are expected of Him to hold our responsibilities in a spirit of service to our society. He looks for us to be faithful, industrious, and honest in the discharge of our duties to both Him and our associates. We are accountable to Him for our actions.

Those who can show themselves faithful in the simple possession of small assets will soon be rewarded with ever-greater responsibilities. Many people are never entrusted with much wealth simply because they are wasteful of the little they had in the first place. Too many live on credit, deep in debt.

Whatever does come into our possession is not to be grasped and hoarded for our own selfish ends. It is appropriate and proper for us to provide adequately for our own families. We are not to be foolish in squandering what has been entrusted to our care on those who try to con us into curious schemes or false and extravagant projects. We are not to be so indulgent of others in need that we neglect to provide for our own people, and so become indebted to others for our own support. We are not to be idle and indolent even if we have the unusual capacity to earn wealth easily and quickly.

What Christ calls us to do as His followers is to be cheerful, good-willed stewards who hold whatever He has entrusted to us in open, generous hands. We are to be compassionate, warmhearted people who are ready and eager to share what we manage with others in genuine need. He told us we would always have poor people in society. The hungry, the forlorn, the lonely, the sick, and the suffering would always be a part of the human scene. To all such we are to be willing to come bearing bread and water in one hand and the good news of His Gospel, supernatural bread and water for the spirit, in the other hand.

This is how He lived. This is how He shared with others. This is how He gave what He possessed for the benefit of those around Him. He ministered as a servant to those whose lives He touched.

To live as He lived in very practical, down-to-earth terms calls for a deliberate sacrifice of some of our possessions. They simply must be made totally available to His purposes upon the planet. What we give, if it is to be truly sacrificial, is much more than the mere tenth of our income, the well-known "tithe." It must far exceed what we consider the surplus over and above our legitimate needs. It must cost us something severe in personal self-sacrifice. We do not and cannot live in the lap of luxury and extravagant comfort while claiming to be sacrificing our assets for others.

To truly be able to share our possessions abundantly with those in need demands that we ourselves shall live in simplicity, doing without the finery and frills. We shall demonstrate joyous self-discipline in our own demands and desires for self-gratification. We shall be glad to do without extravagant expenditures or wasteful practices that impoverish other people.

In this way we can come to count the cost of truly following the Master in a world which for the most part urges us to live only for self-gratification. We will discover that there is deep delight in doing for others. We will find satisfaction in helping the poor and unfortunate. We will sense that our simple service is aligned with the majestic will and purpose of Christ for the planet. Caught up with Him in this work, even our most humble efforts will take on an element of dignity, honor, and adventure that is an inspiration.

As we honor Him in this way, He in turn honors us. To our constant surprise He pours into our lives and experience all that we can pour out on others. There flows from our hearts, our hands, our homes an ever-swelling stream of blessing and goodwill to others. That is the abundant life in Christ flowing out freely from us to refresh and enrich our weary old world.

4

A Renewed Allegiance

Each of us wishes to belong! A profound, powerful impulse buried deep within the human spirit constrains each of us to identify ourselves with some group in society which provides us with the sense of security, support, and sameness so essential to human happiness. In essence we are gregarious people who, though we may pride ourselves in being different in small ways, actually choose to conform to the crowd in the main concepts of life.

Were this not the case, we could not be led. It is the general willingness of human beings to conform that enables them to be marshaled and manipulated en masse by those who wield power and influence over them. There really is such a thing as the "mass mind," which if shaped to either noble or evil ends permits a people to indulge in either lofty pursuits or the most destructive practices.

All social relationships, whether sublime or sordid, have a compelling command over the private individual. They inevitably exert an enormous pressure upon the person to be a part of the process. And they ultimately shape his or her lifestyle. Being one of the group is so compelling that people forfeit their independence in order to become fully integrated into society. They allow not only their conduct but even their thought processes and social mores to be shaped by their own culture.

Next to our self-importance, our personal careers, and our private possessions, we consider our own social status as one of great significance. This explains why people are so proud of their social relationships. It is why they are so keen to discover their "roots." It is why they love to parade their connections and strut their stuff on the stage of social life. It is why some are so ferociously loyal to their family. It is why, as a society, we speak so much about "togetherness."

Yet the startling and truly astonishing thing is that amid all of this intense dedication to our human attachments Christ comes to us and calls us into a supreme and overriding commitment to Himself. His declarations concerning our devotion to Himself more often than not cut across our family ties and social identity. To follow Him implies that a great part of the price will entail disengaging ourselves from the teachings and traditions which formerly provided us with a sense of security and support. There has to come a distinct and definite break with a culture in which we may have felt comfortable but which was at cross-purposes with His way, His truth, His life.

For too long, for far too long, the contemporary twentieth-century church has failed to be forthright, honest, and open in challenging its people to face the formidable call of Christ to be a "called-out" group. All through the entire history of God's dealing with the human race, the chief prerequisite for coming under His gracious care was a willingness to part ways with the world's society. His people were to be distinct, different, and set apart from their contemporaries in a definite, conspicuous allegiance to Himself. Again and again the challenge rings out: "Who will be on the Lord's side?" "Choose ye this day whom you will serve!" "Why halt ye between two opinions? If the Lord be God, follow Him."

Many modern Christian leaders induce their audiences to believe that to become a Christian implies little more than merely coming into another social club. They insinuate that the cost of joining the local church really is no greater than that of joining the local service club. You simply go through the basic introductory rites, pay your fees (the week's collection), then settle in happily to be one of the boys or another of the ladies. It is as if becoming a Christian is simply another social activity added to the long list of other social relationships already enjoyed.

A Renewed Allegiance / 33

The astonishing truth is that Christ calls us to sacrifice any and all social relationships which in any way might diminish or deflect our undivided love and loyalty to Himself. This is a tough order indeed, and it is scarcely mentioned in most pulpits. Our leaders dare not declare that single-minded, strong-willed devotion to Christ will cut off our comfortable accommodation to our corrupt culture. They simply refuse to suggest that to honor Christ will cost us derision and hatred from a cynical society.

The Master was never silent on such issues. He declared openly and without apology, "If they [the society of men] have hated me, they will hate you also!" He never tried to evade the fact that it was not popular to be His follower. But He went much farther than even that. He called on those who desired to belong to His own select company to take drastic steps in disassociating themselves from the comfortable family circle which formerly supported them. Some of His statements shatter all our ideas of the sacredness of family ties and social traditions.

> Everyone that hath forsaken houses, or brethren, or sisters, or father, or mother, or wife, or children, or lands for my name's sake shall receive an hundredfold and shall inherit everlasting life. But

> many that are first shall be last, and the last shall be first" (Matthew 19:29,30).

This is all explosive! It is the call to drastic decisions that fracture family life and call us to tough choices at high costs.

Because of the soft, insipid teaching so current in the church and Christian circles, many of God's people will go to almost any length to find some sort of easy accommodation with their families. They will not take a bold stand in loyalty to Christ. They fear they will alienate their children, parents, or other family members. Rather than dare to be true to Christ they softly submit to the pressure of their peers.

This really is astonishing when we pause to consider the atrocious quality of life and decadence of character so common in many Western families today. In our corrupt culture, home is no longer a haven of repose from the stresses and strains of society. Instead, the loose liaison of men and women dominated by lust and debauchery produces an appalling environment of discord and distrust in which lives and personalities are torn with sorrow and shattered with despair. Broken homes, broken hearts, and broken hopes are the seedbed from which springs so much cynicism and skepticism in our so-called smart and sophisticated society.

Christ calls us to forsake this sort of forlorn and false family association. He calls us

A Renewed Allegiance / 35

with a ringing call to a lofty life of wholesomeness, holiness, and purity of thought as well as action. He expects us to be different in a deep and distinct dimension of definite separation from our associates. He asks us to be willing to sacrifice sordid social relationships in order to be devoted to His pure purposes even at the cost of isolation.

This high cost extends far beyond our own private, immediate, flesh-and-blood families. It embraces also the broader "family of man" as that term applies to the whole of human society. When Christ was among us He spoke specifically regarding the deep alienation that would come to those who were loyal to Him. Read carefully Matthew 10:28-42. There is scarcely a Christian family in the country today which has not known the pain referred to on those pages. Nor has Christ glossed over the great cost of giving our loyal allegiance to Himself!

How can it be otherwise if in fact we are determined to do His will and set our souls to serve His purposes? We immediately become individuals who, as He said, are in the world (the society of man) *but not of it*. In the darkness and decadence of our day He calls us to be the light of His illumination. Amid the corruption of our culture and the putrefaction of our perishing and permissive society He calls us to be the salt of His salvation.

Only His abundant, spontaneous, overcoming life manifest in us as individuals can counteract all the despair and defilement around us. It is His presence which dispels the darkness, His power which overpowers the pollution of our generation.

This does not mean that we disassociate ourselves completely from our contemporaries. It does not mean that we withdraw into cozy, safe little enclaves within the church where our lily-white hands will never be contaminated by contact with the corruption around us. It does not mean that we withdraw from the tears and trauma of our tortured world. No! A thousand times, *no*!

Like Christ—empowered by His presence, constrained by His compassion, and enlivened by His overflowing life—we shall be those who in strength and loving concern reach out to lift the fallen. We shall release the prisoner bound in his own dungeon of self-depredation. We shall bring sight to the blind groping in the darkness of despair. We shall be those who bear the beauty and wonder of Christ's life and love into a wretched old world gone wrong.

When Jesus moved among us as a man, God incarnate in human form, He was scorned and scoffed at as "the friend of publicans and sinners." It was a title He rejoiced to own, for every such life that He touched He transformed. He did not hesitate to move among the lost, the lonely, the least of human beings. It was sinners He had come to call. It was lost sheep He had come to find and to save. His own character was never tarnished by contact with the defiled and despised. His own person was never polluted with picking up the perishing.

The simple reason was because of His own deep, distinct difference. He was truth in the midst of deception. He was life in the midst of death. He was light in the midst of dread human despair.

He sacrificed His own social relationship to save others.

He asks us to do the same even at the cost of being considered eccentrics by our astonished associates and fanatics by our detractors.

He stated categorically that His brothers and His sisters, even His mother, were not those of human family ties but those who without hesitation did His bidding. It is thus that we are drawn into the family of God. It is in this way that we become identified with Him as our dearest Friend, and God Himself becomes our most precious parent, our Father!

5

Our High and Noble Calling

Humility is not the hallmark of our Western world. We are a proud, proud people!

A powerful haughtiness pervades our society. We parade an intellectual arrogance that is truly astonishing. We are known the world over for our abrasive attitude of superiority. Even in spiritual matters we often behave as though we are a cut above other cultures.

All the traditional arguments advanced to support our so-called superior lifestyle are well-known. We have been taught from infancy that we possess the finest political system ever devised for man. We are sure our educational systems provide the most sophisticated enlightenment ever known. We boast about having the highest standard of living in the world.

And in Christian endeavors, whatever form they take, we parade our programs and projects as though they were of superior spiritual quality. We have deluded ourselves into believing that our scientific skills, modern technology, and high-powered business methods, if applied to the church, can usher

Our High and Noble Calling / 39

in the kingdom of God on a grand worldwide scale. The proud shout of the twentieth-century church is to reach the whole world for Christ in our generation. It is always assumed that this will be accomplished by means of mass communication: literature, radio, television, films, records, aircraft, satellites, and computer technology.

All of the above somehow excite us tremendously. With our materialistic mind-set we quickly get caught up in any movement of this magnitude. We assume rather naively that, given enough money, men, and skilled management, we can make any mission a success. So we call great conventions, assemble huge sums of financial support, set out special so-called spiritual strategies, and then go out to accomplish our aims in the world, assuming that the projects will astonish everyone.

All of this panders precisely to those aspects of our individual lives which were discussed in the preceding chapters. Because of our backgrounds we find it compelling to cater to our own selfish self-interests. Here we can promote our own careers and advance our own interests. Grandiose church schemes can be a display for wealth, power, and influence because of our affluence. And in all this we find fertile ground in which to cultivate our social relationships and parade our personal contacts with celebrities.

In the face of all this excitement it is sobering to hear Christ tell us that the kingdom of

God is really not of such human design at all. It is not an outward demonstration of power, influence, or strategy displayed in tangible terms that are measured by our five fallible senses. Rather, He states categorically that it is the secret inner process of spiritual reorientation which goes on within a human soul that has received Him as the Most High Majesty.

The absolute bedrock requirement needed for this to happen is a simplicity of spirit and humility of heart akin to that of a small child. Jesus actually picked up a tiny tot one day, held the youngster snugly in His strong arms, and declared without apology:

> I say unto you, Except ye be converted and become as little children, ye shall not enter into the kingdom of heaven. Whosoever therefore shall humble himself as this little child, the same is greatest in the kingdom of heaven (Matthew 18:3,4).

In our Western world we simply do not want to talk about humility. We are self-centered people who are proud of our professions, proud of our achievements, proud of our possessions, proud of even our spiritual stature. Millions of modern Christians boast of their special church affiliations. They are urged to parade their special spiritual

Our High and Noble Calling / 41

gifts. They flaunt their biblical knowledge and pose as somewhat superspiritual individuals in society.

It is not surprising that all of this is an affront to God our Father. He simply is not impressed. As ever of old, He looks for men and women broken in spirit and contrite in heart (will) who seek Him in utter penitence. It is with such souls that He delights to reside. But this will never happen unless there is genuine repentance from pride, profound remorse for our perverseness, and relinquishment of our sordid pollution.

When John the Baptist, the greatest man born of a woman, came as Christ's forerunner he preached the absolute need for repentance. When Christ started out on His public ministry He called for repentance. When the apostles of the early church arrested the attention of their society they demanded repentance. Yet the Christian leaders of our generation are almost silent on the subject. They are reluctant to carry out Christ's clear command that repentance and remission of sins should be preached in His name among all the nations of the earth. Read Luke 24:45-48.

The question needs to be asked clearly and very emphatically: "What is repentance from God's viewpoint? What does it demand of man?"

It is absolutely essential for laypeople

to understand this. If there is to be harmony, unity, and goodwill between the Living Christ and us common men and women, it must be based not only on the majestic accomplished work of Christ but also on our personal willingness to repent of our pride, our perverseness, and our pollution.

In essence repentance is a disclosure to us of our undone condition before the absolute love, purity, justice, and incandescent righteousness of the Risen Christ. It is borne in upon our stained souls so smeared with selfishness, our spirits so sullied with pride, our daily behavior so corrupted with evil that we are at odds with God our Father. *We actually become very acutely aware that we have set ourselves up in antagonism to Him.* We are at enmity with God. We are rebels living in open defiance of His best intentions for us. We have set ourselves up in pride as supreme in our own affairs. So we refuse to receive Him as Monarch in our lives. We close Him out of our considerations. We live as though He were dead.

The actual truth is just the opposite: He declares *us* to be dead in our sins and iniquities, needing desperately to cast ourselves upon His mercy in profound repentance and beseeching Him to impart His divine and eternal life to us.

Repentance, if it is genuine, arises from a deep and profound conviction by Christ's Spirit that we are indeed wrongdoers who in sinister sin against Him have become alienated from Him. Though in His wondrous grace, generosity, and love He extends to us His mercy, forgiveness, and acceptance on the basis of His own magnanimous self-sacrifice, He *demands* that we for our part turn from our wicked ways, repent of our wrongs, seek His companionship, and claim His amazing justification through total forgiveness.

Repentance is not a once-for-all experience that takes place only at the time of initial conversion. It is in fact a daily sacrifice in which we see ourselves as we really are in the white, intense light of Christ's character and His Word, so that we need to turn to Him for cleansing and for forgiveness. It is the continual repudiation of evil in our lives. It is the humble admission of having missed the mark in the high calling to which Christ calls us. It is the bold willingness to face our sins and to come to hate them with utter disdain and stern intensity because they are such a grief to Christ and such a corruption of our own characters.

Such repentance drives us to our knees. It starts our tears. It wrings the desperate inner cry of the spirit from us: "O God in Christ, be merciful to me a sinner!"

When we examine the Biblical record of God dealing with men who walked with Him in close communion, it is remarkable to discover how they were driven to repentance: righteous Job of old; David, a monarch after God's own heart; Isaiah, the great prophet; Peter, the flaming apostle. All were individuals who, when they saw with inner clarity their own undone condition, were stricken with acute remorse and cried out in repentance for restoration.

In our own age, every great spiritual awakening that has occurred anywhere in the world has been marked with genuine repentance. In response to the entreaty of God's people for renewal of supernatural work in their midst, Christ has come by His own Spirit to perform a sovereign work of conviction among Christians and non-Christians. No longer must people be persuaded that they are in need of salvation. Instead they are made acutely aware that they stand undone in the overwhelming presence of The Holy One. In deep contrition they humble themselves before His Person and cry out in earnestness for His mercy, His cleansing, His pardon, His acceptance.

The world with all its self-deception and facetious cynicism will scoff at anyone who chooses to follow Christ in contrition of spirit. They will laugh loud and long at the person who sets himself to do Christ's bidding in lowliness of mind. They will demean the man or woman brave enough to part ways with the crowd in humble service and loving loyalty to His Majesty, the Lord Jesus

Christ. They will ostracize the individual who above all else, in genuine repentance, comes under the control of Christ, allowing Him to establish His kingdom within their soul.

To the world—so proud, so perverse, so polluted—the life of purity, uprightness, integrity, justice, and mercy to which Christ calls us is all utterly impractical and an irritation. It simply does not make sense to men and women who despise righteousness and revel in iniquity. They call good evil and evil they laughingly call good.

For the true child of God, called of Christ into His companionship, introduced into the family of the Father, and sealed by God's Spirit into a new citizenship in a new kingdom from above, the world system becomes foreign territory. We no longer feel at home or at ease in the contemporary scene. This world is now no longer our permanent residence. We discern in a profound and powerful way that we have altered our allegiance by giving it to Christ and His eternal kingdom. We have assumed the status of strangers, nonresident aliens, pilgrims passing through the shifting scenes of our ever-changing, skeptical society. Here there is nothing stable, nothing sure, nothing secure.

We have found a brand-new center for life, and that center is Christ. It is Him whom we love above all else with unswerving loyalty. It is Him whom we serve in unflinching faith.

The world will call us mad eccentrics. He will call us His own precious people!

*This booklet
has been excerpted from W. Phillip Keller's
compelling call to follow Christ
in these perilous times:*

Predators in Our Pulpits

Bestselling author W. Phillip Keller explains why "The greatest threat to the church of Jesus Christ today is not from without, but from its own leadership within." Writing to every Christian layperson, Keller censures Christian leadership for its lack of pure, biblical teaching and urgently encourages Christians to recognize their own inadequacies and sinful lives.

He addresses such critical issues as: Why are we hearing less and less of the true gospel message? and Are our leaders guiding us to an authentic relationship with Christ, or are many merely providing balm for everyday life?

*Available at
Christian bookstores everywhere*

W. PHILLIP KELLER was born and raised in Kenya and educated in the United States, England, and Canada. He is the author of 39 books in 26 foreign languages, including *A Shepherd Looks at Psalm 23*.

Dear Reader:

We would appreciate hearing from you regarding this Harvest House pocket book. It will enable us to continue to give you the best in Christian publishing.

1. What most influenced you to purchase *The Secret of His Presence*?
   - ☐ Author
   - ☐ Subject matter
   - ☐ Backcover copy
   - ☐ Recommended
   - ☐ Cover/Title
   - ☐ _____

2. Your overall rating of this book:
   ☐ Excellent ☐ Very good ☐ Good ☐ Fair ☐ Poor

3. How likely would you be to purchase other books by this author?
   - ☐ Very likely
   - ☐ Somewhat likely
   - ☐ Not very likely
   - ☐ Not at all

4. After reading this Harvest House Pocket Book would you be inclined to purchase the complete book, *Predators in Our Pulpits*?
   ☐ Yes ☐ No

5. What types of books most interest you? (check all that apply)
   - ☐ Women's Books
   - ☐ Marriage Books
   - ☐ Current Issues
   - ☐ Self Help/Psychology
   - ☐ Bible Studies
   - ☐ Fiction
   - ☐ Biographies
   - ☐ Children's Books
   - ☐ Youth Books
   - ☐ Other _____

6. Please check the box next to your age group.
   - ☐ Under 18
   - ☐ 18-24
   - ☐ 25-34
   - ☐ 35-44
   - ☐ 45-54
   - ☐ 55 and over

Mail to: Editorial Director
Harvest House Publishers
1075 Arrowsmith
Eugene, OR 97402

Name _____

Address _____

City _____ State _____ Zip _____

Thank you for helping us to help you in future publications!